MW01487463

A Drop in the Bucket

Thoughts, Musings, and Jottings on Life's Experiences

By

LARRY BEIGHEY

FORWARD BY

Newt Gingrich

Bloomington, IN Milton Keynes, UK

authorHOUSE™

AuthorHouse™
1663 Liberty Drive, Suite 200
Bloomington, IN 47403
www.authorhouse.com
Phone: 1-800-839-8640

AuthorHouse™ UK Ltd.
500 Avebury Boulevard
Central Milton Keynes, MK9 2BE
www.authorhouse.co.uk
Phone: 08001974150

First published by AuthorHouse
4/5/2006

ISBN: 1-4259-2298-8 (sc)

Printed in the United States of America
Bloomington, Indiana

This book is printed on acid-free paper.

Cover design and layout by Rick Sargent.

FIRST EDITION
FIRST PRINTING

FORWARD

By

NEWT GINGRICH

I am honored to write an introduction for Larry Beighey's book because he literally changed my life in two very important ways.

First, through his daughter, Anne, he gave me an extraordinary associate who made my work much more effective and enjoyable as House Republican Whip, Speaker of the House, and then as a businessman and civic leader after leaving the House. The values, intensity, enthusiasm, and determination Anne brings to life are a great tribute to both her mom and dad. Their values and their commitment to life are reflected in their daughter's career.

Second, when I entered the private sector in 1999, I visited with Larry to learn his secrets as an entrepreneur. One key lesson he taught me was "never be afraid to ask too much or offer too little." Free enterprise is a process of getting to a mutually acceptable agreement in which both parties feel they are better off because they were able to accomplish something they could not get done on their own.

Larry emphasized that in negotiating you were supposed to represent your own interests. If you had offered too little you could always raise the offer when it was rejected. If you had asked for too much you could always lower the price as the conversation continued.

Larry insisted that if you offered too much the other person would of course accept it but you might have paid much more than you needed to. If you asked for too little the other side would of course accept it but then you would have received much less than you might have.

I found this process of pleasantly and firmly representing your own interests inside your own head fascinating. Larry asserted that most people lacked the nerve to calmly represent themselves and tended to almost automatically offer too much or ask for too little. They wanted to be pleasant and to be accepted more than they wanted the best deal.

Larry's insights will help you learn a lot more about being an effective entrepreneur and a profitable businessman or woman. More importantly, Larry's stories and the principles they illustrate will help you live a better life and be a better person. Larry understands full well that life is about much more than simply making money.

Larry has lived a life devoted to his family, his community, and to Penn State. One of the happiest events we had when I was Speaker was when Coaches Joe Paterno and Lou Holtz came to speak for me at a Georgia Fundraiser. Larry is a devoted Penn State fan and was excited to be asked to introduce Joe Paterno to the 500 people present. He and Coach Paterno had a great time together. I could see the joy Larry got from his long relationship with his alma mater. It was one more mark of the enthusiastic and complete person he is.

This book will teach you lessons about business but more importantly it will teach you lessons about life.

When you are done you will feel you have made a new friend and his name is Larry.

Newt Gingrich,
Speaker of the U.S. House of Representatives, 1995-1998
Founder, The Center for Health Transformation

to

JAC & MARTHA BEIGHEY
WHO MADE IT ALL POSSIBLE

ACKNOWLEDGEMENTS

I wish to thank many people for their input and untiring support over the years it took to complete *A Drop in the Bucket.*

To my mother and father, Jac and Martha Beighey, who gave me many lessons in life. Many of the *Drops* in this book come from their teachings. They taught me the joys of life and encouraged me to continue to advance my learning. It was never a question of *if* I was going to college, but *where* I was going to college. I was the first member of my family in any generation to go to college. I regret that they did not live to see my book in print.

To my three sons, Skip, Tom and Tim Beighey, and three daughters, Susan Morrell, Elizabeth Miller and Anne Woodbury and their husbands, Dave, Jason and Jeff, for their encouragement, advice and help in getting this book into print ... they certainly have heard these "Pearls" enough times.

I want to especially recognize Megan Head Meehan, Elizabeth Beighey Miller, Anne Beighey Woodbury and Jeff Woodbury for their valued input and editing of my book.

Many thanks to other family members and friends, who cheered me on and offered encouragement, suggestions and advice throughout the long years it took to write this book.

I struggled to choose a book name and received over a dozen suggestions from family and friends. Susan Beighey Morrell, my daughter, finally hit on *A Drop in the Bucket*.

Special thanks, Rick Sargent, for the cover design, artwork and layout. Rick came up with the caricature of "The Thinker" and incorporated it into an ingenious book cover. Thank you, Rick, for your work and permission to use it in *A Drop in the Bucket*.

One of the *Drops* in this book is "Ask a Busy Person." It says: *"If you want to get something done, give it to a busy person. A busy person always seems to find time to add something else to their list of things to do."* Of course, this busy person is Newt Gingrich. (www.newt.org)

I know he is a fully involved and busy person ... but that is just the person who would take time out of his demanding schedule to write such a moving and sincere Forward.

It is with heartfelt gratitude that I thank Newt for the thoughtful Forward to *A Drop in the Bucket*.

Thank you, of course, to my wife, Carole, for her inspirational support, backing and assistance. Most importantly, I thank her for always believing in me and giving me that final push I needed to publish my work. As the author of her own book series, *The Waddodles of Hollow Lake* (www.waddodles.com), she appreciates the hard work that goes into such an effort as writing a book. Thank you, Carole. "I love you ... Forever, Forever."

I have a wonderful feeling of accomplishment for having finished *A Drop in the Bucket*. I loved writing it and hope the "Drops" will be well received by those who read them.

Larry Beighey
November, 2005

INTRODUCTION

My business career was like a roller coaster. There were many ups and downs, from being President of a large corporation … to losing my job when the company was sold … to buying a troubled plastic bucket company and turning it into a successful, lucrative business.

During all of this and the day-to-day life of raising six children with my wife, Carole, I relied on my beliefs, feelings and judgments to guide me along the way.

I started to accumulate my thoughts and sayings early on in my business career – I always had the notion it was succinct and clever to put some of life's messages in the form of a saying or phrase.

I never thought about how many phrases I had accumulated, but recently when I started to write them down, I found I had close to 100.

As far as I know, each insight is a product of my own thinking, my own words and my own experiences. In the case where someone gave a thought to me, I have given them the credit.

Bottles and buckets played an important part in my life - thus the name, *A Drop in the Bucket*. Each of these "Drops" tells a meaningful lesson that played a significant role in my personal, business, family and social life.

The book is not meant to be read at one sitting; rather, it is a book that you can pick up and read one or several "Drops" ... returning at some later time to read more.

I hope you find "*A Drops in the Bucket*" useful and that one of these "Drops" will strike a chord and benefit you in some way.

Larry Beighey
LJBeighey@aol.com
November, 2005

TABLE OF CONTENS

Board Room to Boiler Room

One of the things I always prided myself on was a conscientious effort and ability to adapt to my surroundings. I have noticed and observed many people who were able to talk to one group of people and totally unable to speak to another group.

Jokingly, I would say that I was equally comfortable in the boardroom or the boiler room. It is important and, in fact, essential that when you're dealing with other people, the sincerity of your voice and your actions make other people comfortable with you.

How many times have you seen or observed someone who, by their actions or the way they were dressed, made another party uncomfortable to be around them?

It takes a conscientious effort and real, solid sincerity on your part to make the other party comfortable. It is important that you are adaptable enough to win people over – no matter what kind of environment you are in.

A Clean Desktop –
Under Worked or Overpaid?

When I was starting my business career, I was very organized since my education was as an industrial engineer. My desk was always very neat and organized when I left work at the end of the business day.

One day, an old-timer who had been around my company for many years told me "a clean desktop means you are under worked or overpaid." To me, it was an unintelligent remark that is contrary to my education and my thinking.

I have always felt that everything should be well organized and in its proper place.

Throughout my business life, I have used a simple organizational system. I have a few files to keep myself organized. My system utilizes files named IN, OUT, FILE and ATTENTION. When mail came in I would put it in the IN file until I had a chance to go through it. Following the timesaving tip of only touching mail once, I would decide what to do with it the first time

I went through it. I would mark on it what action or routing to take and label it appropriately OUT, FILE or ATTENTION. OUT to send it on its way. FILE if I wanted to keep it under my filing system ... I always kept an outline of my file folders to refer to and determine where I wanted to file it. My ATTENTION file was an alphabetical accordion folder where I would file things that I had to take action on later. To this day, I still use this same system.

If You Can't Say Anything Good, Don't Say Anything At All

I think it was Will Rogers who said, "if you can't say anything good about somebody, then don't say anything at all." I wish I had said it because it is so true and expresses something that I am constantly trying to overcome. It is a continuous battle to not "go negative" about someone or something they said or did.

It doesn't serve any useful purpose for you to go negative, and it is hurtful and insensitive to do this. Instead, simply make positive comments or no comment at all.

I think it was in about 5 BC (Before Carole), when I was a "swinging bachelor," that I had an embarrassing experience that stuck with me the rest of my life.

A cute girl that I always wanted to date finally broke up with the fellow she had been going with for a long time. I quickly seized on the opportunity and asked her out. Of course, while on the date she asked me what I thought of Mr. You-Know-Who. I was less than flattering in my opinion of him and didn't hesitate to tell her what I thought. Of course, a short time later they got back together and I lost two friends. Lesson learned!

In no place is this lesson truer than in politics. You must be careful what you say about a colleague.

I could never be a politician … I am too inflexible. I discussed this one time with a close adviser to Speaker Newt Gingrich. I asked him how a politician could be so outspoken about someone's position and later be all chummy with them. He told me that it was "not personal … just business." You must be compromising because "today's adversary could be tomorrow's needed vote or supporter."

If you observe most successful politicians, they will differ vehemently on the issues but are very careful not to attack personally.

So remember, "If you can't say anything good, don't say anything at all."

4

Bottomed Out

Did you ever have days when everything seems to go wrong ... those days when things get worse as the day goes on. I have experienced many of these types of days throughout my personal and business career. Like most people, I would complain about it to everyone and anyone who would listen – but I came to realize that no one really wants to hear about all your problems and worries.

My realization came from a vivid real-life experience that I had during the energy crisis of 1976. I was the Energy Czar for Brockway Glass Company. Brockway had drilled gas wells and had built a gathering system to pipe the gas over to the natural gas supplier. During the crisis, the gas company confiscated our gas and would not deliver it to our plants. Since glass manufacturing is an energy-intensive industry and we could not get enough natural gas, we had to shut the plants down and lay off all the people. We had only enough gas to keep the glass in the furnaces molten; there was not enough energy to manufacture any glass containers.

Every morning at 7 AM, I would have an emergency meeting with the President of the Glass Container Division to review where and how much energy we had so we could determine what our Emergency Operating Plan would be for that day. Since it was my job to procure the energy for the glass factories, I was under intense pressure and had many problems and worries.

Naturally, I would tell my "tale of woe" to anyone who would listen. During one of the worst mornings of the crisis, I was in the men's room when a co-worker walked in. He was a happy-go-lucky eight-to-fiver who liked to tell stories, shoot the breeze and gossip. He asked me, "How you doing?" I started to unload on him about all my woes and worries. Well, he hurriedly washed his hands and bolted out the door ... he couldn't wait to get away from me.

It hit me like a ton of bricks that people really did not care or want to hear about your problems. From that day on, I have tried not to burden people with my worries and problems and found that the best approach when someone asks you, "How are you doing today?" is to simply grit your teeth and reply "I have bottomed out ... I'm on the way back ... I'm doing fine."

Cream Always Rises to the Top

Years ago, you could buy milk that was pasteurized or homogenized. Back in those days, milk only came in glass bottles … milk cartons had not been developed yet. Many people would buy the pasteurized milk since it was cheaper then the homogenized milk. Do you remember pasteurized milk? In a glass bottle, you could see a layer of cream above the milk. Before you opened the milk bottle you had to shake it up vigorously to mix the cream with the milk. When you would put it back into storage and let it sit long enough, that cream would always separate back to the top, with the milk underneath it.

Pasteurized milk is very much like human behavior. If you take someone with hidden talent and give them the opportunity, eventually their talent will rise to the top – just like with pasteurized milk.

Carole and I made a decision that we would not move our children once they were past the eighth grade. I had been in a position where I had seen families move around frequently and saw the influence it had on their children's confidence and education. I turned down several promotions because it would have violated the trust our six children had placed in us to watch out for their well-being and education. Perhaps it hindered my advancement, but in the long run it all worked out.

We had about a five-year window between our first four children being out of high school and before the last two entered high school.

When the window opened, I went to the President of the company and told him I was ready to move if it would advance my career goal of being a Division President before the age of 50. He told me he would "put it in his hip pocket," and at some point would get back to me. About two years later, we were on our way to Atlanta, Georgia, where we lived until I retired.

One of the obstacles we expected to encounter was the education of our two youngest children. We were sure that we would have to put our children in private school, but thought we would try the public school first. After one year, our daughters did not want to leave their school and go to a private school. Believing that the "cream always rises to the top," we kept them in public school. We made the right decision.

Our daughter Elizabeth graduated with honors in her high school class. She went on to receive her degree from Penn State and achieved a middle management position with TBS Broadcasting, later to become Time Warner. She is now a stay-at-home mom with her two small children and a full-time Creative Memories Consultant with 17 consultants working under her.

Daughter Anne graduated high school as the "Outstanding Student." She went on to Penn State and started to work as a summer intern in 1992 for Newt Gingrich before he became the Speaker of the House of Representatives ... the rest of her career is told by the Former Speaker in the forward to this book. She is now a Senior Vice-President of Fleishman-Hillard in Washington, D.C. and specializes in the health care field. She has co-authored a book with Newt Gingrich entitled *Saving Lives and Saving Money.*

Not bad for two products of the public school system.

The moral of the story is that people often do not reach their full potential, but if you give them enough time and instill in them some self-confidence, eventually their talent will come out.

Just like pasteurized milk, an individual's "cream will always rise to the top."

I Met God

It was a dark, rainy night when I met God. It was not the first time I met Him … As I mentioned in the Drop on "Meditation," I prayed and meditated in a business men's church group every week day for over 10 years. I still pray and meditate every day, all be it, not always in church but as I am exercising. I feel so cleansed mentally and physically when I am finished with my routine.

My communication with God had been through meditation and prayer but the most significant emotional event of His power and all knowing and caring presence was the night I met him face to face.

I was driving home from a late night meeting at my plant. It was about a 35-40 minute drive from the plant to my home. It was a terrible stormy night with lots of rain, sleet, thunder and lighting. I was traveling on the perimeter Interstate 285 around Atlanta, Georgia in the storm when my car had a tire "blowout." I quickly worked my way over to the edge of the road and stopped.

I called AAA and was informed that, because of the bad weather, it would be a four-hour wait before they could get to me. Here I was stranded in a storm in my business suit and tie with a flat tire. I didn't know what to do!

I noticed an exit a few hundred yards ahead so I decided to slowly work my way to and down the exit. I didn't want to leave my car on the Interstate over night so I figured I could make my way down the exit and be in a better position to think thru my options.

As I sat pondering what I was going to do, a jeep pulled up behind me with a 30ish guy with a beard behind the wheel. He got out in the driving rain and started to walk towards my car. I was scared and hid my wallet under the seat … I didn't know what he might do so I had my guard up.

I rolled down my window and he asked me what was wrong. I told him I had a flat tire. He said, "Do you have an umbrella?" I told him I did. He replied, "If you will hold the umbrella for me I will change the tire."

As he was finishing the tire change the rain stopped. I got in the car and retrieved all my cash from my wallet - $80. I figured it was the least I could do for all his efforts.

When he finished I tried several times to give him the money but he just refused. All he said was for me to do a "good deed" for someone else in the future.

I said, "At least tell me your name so I can properly thank you." He said, "You can call me God." He jumped in his Jeep and drove down the road.

I am convinced there is a God and he watches over you and helps you in many ways ... sometimes in very unexpected ways.

It was not the last time I have talked to God but it was the last time I met him face to face.

I now know He is there for me and the next time I see him face to face He will help me on life's journey.

Shuttle Diplomacy

I have always been intrigued with something I learned in the 70's – Shuttle Diplomacy.

The first time I ever heard the term was Henry Kissinger's use of Shuttle Diplomacy between Menachem Begin and Anwar Sadat. Kissinger would "shuttle" between Egypt and Israel, trying to bring peace between the Jews and Arabs. Sadat and Begin had never met until Kissinger had worked out all the details and obstacles between them. The result was the famous flight by Sadat to meet Begin and address the Israel Knesset.

Shuttle diplomacy, or mediated communication, is the use of a third party to convey information back and forth between two parties. The intermediary can provide suggestions and move a conflict toward a resolution.

The next major use of Shuttle Diplomacy that I remember was by President Jimmy Carter. Again, it involved Menachem Begin and Anwar Sadat.

The peace process had stalled, so the President talked both parties into meeting at the secluded and protected Camp David in the Catoctin Mountains in the Maryland hills of the United States. Both parties were in separate compounds at Camp David and never met. President Carter and his team would "shuttle" between the two camps, trying to find some common ground for peace between the two countries. Several times one or the other of the two groups threatened to leave, but still President Carter keep "shuttling" between them. They finally met face to face at the White House and signed the Camp David Accord.

I was very impressed with Shuttle Diplomacy and found it to be very effective in my business negotiations. I discovered that by "shuttling" between two groups or individuals, I could keep them focused on the issues and not have them face-to-face where they were more than likely to "draw a line in the sand." Also, by going back and forth between the two parties, I was the one that decided the length of the meeting.

Shuttle Diplomacy is not the most efficient method of negotiating, but it is very, very effective.

8

Don't Ever Be Embarrassed to Ask Too Much or Offer Too Little

Former Speaker of the House Newt Gingrich, asked me to help him with a business plan when he was making the transition into the business world. I started each section with a little quip that I had used over the years. "Don't ever be embarrassed to ask too much or offer too little" was one of them. He liked it and used it several times in his presentations, always giving me credit.

Americans seem to be embarrassed to make a high or low offer when negotiating. You shouldn't be, as you do not necessarily know all the facts when negotiating and the other party is not going to tell you.

One of our children was buying their first house and I advised her to offer 20% below what the seller was asking. She said, "I am embarrassed to offer that amount … It is an insult to the seller … She will never accept it." The seller's agent said the offer was so ridiculous that she would not present it to the seller. Both the buyer and seller agents worked in the same real estate firm and the buyer's agent took this matter to his manager. The bottom line was that the selling agent left the company and my daughter bought the house at a discounted price – over 15% less than the original asking price.

When we sold our Atlanta house, we asked a very high price for it. Our selling agent said we would never get that much for the house. We stuck to our price! The result: our house sold in two weeks at the highest price any comparable house in the neighborhood had ever sold for. Ironically, that house just went on the market again … the asking price … the same amount they paid six years ago.

In most other countries you are expected to negotiate. Only in the United States do we seem embarrassed to make a low offer or ask a high price. Remember, you do not know what the other party's situation is at the time, and you may end up leaving money on the table. Go for it and "don't ever be embarrassed to ask too much or offer too little."

"Dance With the Girl That Brung Ya"

I have known many successful people in business, politics and other ventures that tried to change their methods after having reached success in their chosen endeavor and experienced disastrous results.

I remember a small bar and grill in the town where I grew up. It was a rundown, homely place that specialized in a "shot and beer" trade, but had very good fare such as hamburgers, fries and other kinds of finger foods. The place was always packed with its regular customers and other people who would venture in late at night for a sandwich and a drink. The owner thought that he could expand his business by remodeling and enlarging his bar and grill to attract a larger, upscale crowd. After spending a great deal of time and money renovating the bar and grill, he saw his business dwindle away to the point that the place was almost always empty. The regulars quit coming because they thought the place was too fancy and the prices too high. The upscale crowd quit coming because the bar and grill had lost its late-night charm.

Robert Woodruff, one of the Coca-Cola founders, understood this principle well. The story goes that Coca-Cola spent a lot of money with an advertising firm on a new product called Diet Coke ... Woodruff famously said "Don't #@!# with the Holy Water" ... They called it Tab. It didn't become Diet Coke until after Woodruff died.

Or, how about Coca-Cola changing the Coke formula after Woodruff was gone? The result – disaster. They finally had to bring back the original formula and call it Coca- Cola Classic. Today, I doubt that you can find a bottle of the revised formula of Coca- Cola, only Coca-Cola Classic.

In these examples, as in many others I have experienced, the individuals should remember the old adage, "dance with the girl that brung ya" or "don't try to change boats in the middle of the stream."

People who have been very successful in their endeavors should remember what made them successful and resist changing their tactics without careful deliberation and analysis of what consequences could lay ahead.

Don't Make Spontaneous Decisions

This little "Pearl" goes along quite nicely with the *Drop* entitled, "Don't Take the Decision Maker."

Many times in life, you have to make a spontaneous decision and then realize that you might have taken another course of action if you'd had time to think about all the options and solutions available to you.

One little trick I learned was to "put it in a drawer for a while." When you are working on a project or situation for a long period of time, your thinking can become jaded and you may make many mistakes; perhaps you should have taken a different path. I found that by putting it away for a while, maybe only overnight, you could take another look at it and refresh your thinking.

Don't Take the Decision Maker

Numerous times in my business career, while in front of a group of people, I would encounter a situation that would require me to make an immediate decision. Many times, my decision would alienate a great number of people. One of the subtle tricks that I learned during this process was "don't take the decision maker."

If the decision maker is not involved in the situation, it is always possible for others to say, "I don't have the authority to make that decision, I will have to get back to you." This does not put the decision maker on the spot and when the subordinate comes to him, he has time to weigh all the options and to make an informed decision.

This is a much better way of handling the situation and gives the decision maker a chance to thoroughly think it through.

Don't Spend Money Until You Have To

Have you ever gone on a spending spree, made impulse purchase decisions or spent money hurriedly and then later regretted it?

I recommend that you don't spend money until you have to. A good example of this might be your desire to buy a new car when your existing automobile is still in great condition and doesn't give you any trouble or cause you any major expense. If you rush out to buy a new car, you will have spent the money before you had to – perhaps you could have put the money to better use for something that you really needed.

A better approach is to annually develop a Capital Spending Priority List. This will enable you to plan your major spending for the year and help you to prioritize your capital spending. Once you have developed your Capital Spending Priority List you can only add something to the list by eliminating something you had previously included in the list. See "A Year of Planned Action" for details on how to develop a Capital Spending Plan and establishing spending priorities. This will help eliminate the urge to "spend money before you have to."

Plant a Seed

"Plant a Seed" is the easiest way to combat "NIH" (Not Invented Here). Over the years, I have found in business or personal relationships that the easiest road to success is to plant the seed of an idea. If you suggest something to someone and it is not their idea, you will often run into resistance.

The best way around this is to suggest something in a broad sense or ask it as a question, in a non-controversial way, so they do not feel that they have been given a directive. Rather, it is perceived as a suggestion or a question. Let it sit for a while and let them mull it around in their minds. Sometime later, bring the subject back up and get their input. They will often have tweaked your idea a little bit, but you will be surprised at how close their comeback is to what you suggested. They have to make some changes or it will not be their idea (NIH).

In my experience, planting a seed will have a very high success rate and you'll have accomplished your goal. After all, what do you care whose idea it was if it accomplishes your goal?

Eventually, everyone will realize whose idea it was and you'll get the credit that you deserve. You will have accomplished your goal, and you'll have accomplished it in a very effective way.

Good Grief

Grief is usually thought of as dark, sad and more often than not, death. I found a great book, *Good Grief*, that has helped me get through many crises and I have shared it with many others.

Good Grief is a little book with a long history! It is about life's experiences, crises and disappointments. It had a big impact on me when I faced difficult times. It is in its 35th Anniversary Edition. It was first published in 1962, based on one chapter from *Minister and Doctor Meet*, written by Granger E. Westberg in 1961. It made its way to me via my daughter, Anne. The chain link was from Senator Connie Mack of Florida, who received it from a friend when Senator Mack's father died … Senator Mack gave it to Speaker Newt Gingrich when his father died … Speaker Gingrich gave it to my daughter, Anne.

The Introduction in *Good Grief* says, "We spend a good portion of our lives working diligently to acquire those things that make life rich and meaningful – friends, a wife or husband, children, a home, a job, material comforts, money (lets face it), and security. What happens to us when we lose any of these persons or things which are so important to us?"

We grieve over the loss of anything important. The Introduction goes on to say, "We certainly mean to include grief related to death in this discussion; but we can observe the same grief process at work in many other kinds of losses as well." Grief can come from many sources, including, but not limited to a move, divorce, loss of a job, being laid off, passed over for a promotion, loss of health, accidents or financial ruin. Any of these things can set off a cycle of grief. Grief is a part of life.

Good Grief supports the idea that the grief process tends to follow a pattern of stages ...10 stages. The book says, "The 10 stages of grief must be understood to be the normal process through which most people must go as they face up to their loss ... every person does not necessarily go through all these 10 stages, nor does a person necessarily go through them in this order. Moreover, it is impossible to differentiate clearly between each of these stages, for a person never moves neatly from one stage to the other."

The Book goes on to say, "... various forms of loss ... need not be entirely damaging; they can ... also be life-enhancing. Suffering is not good, but you need not be devastated by it. Ultimately, we can be healed by our bitterness and move ahead."

I hope you find this little book useful. It is an easy read but packs a powerful message.

15

Firm and Fair – Tough Love

Many years ago, I had a discussion with my father, Jac Beighey, about what it takes to be a good father and a good boss. My father had been a supervisor in a large rubber factory and he had spent most of my young, impressionable life in management, and along with my mother, raised my sister and me.

In one of our many discussions, I asked him why he was such a good manager and was so well liked by his subordinates and peers. He told me to always remember one simple rule: Be firm and fair.

He told me that people respected someone who is fair and takes a stand on any issue. He likened this too "tough love." It is not always easy to discipline your children or a subordinate, but in the end they will respect you for being "firm and fair."

I've always tried to strive to live up to this "rule" in all situations, be it raising our six children or being a good business leader.

Ask a Busy Person

If you want to get something done, give it to a busy person.

A busy person always seems to find time to add something else to their long list of things to do. Conversely, others, who have much less to do, never seem to get anything done.

Busy people have organized and prioritized their tasks. This allows them to get much more accomplished and have room to take on additional projects.

Good in Every Bad

THE BEST DAY OF MY LIFE

I have always believed that no matter how bad a situation is you can always look and find a bright spot in it. Read the following account of an event that happened to me and I think you will agree "There is Good in Every Bad."

During 1969 and 1970, I was working for Brockway Glass Company as the Director of Training. My job was to travel to each of the 13 factories throughout the United States each month and teach Management Principles to Front-line Supervisors. It was a hectic schedule that required me to spend a couple days a month in each of the 13 factories. I was only home about three days per month, including weekends, which was about enough time to pick up clean laundry.

My schedule took me across the country ... from Freehold, New Jersey to Oakland, California, with many stops along the way. Then I would start the cycle all over again. This program went on for about 15 or 16 months.

I didn't mind the schedule since I was a 31-year-old bachelor with a 1967 Corvette Stingray, living in my parent's home in a basement apartment in DuBois, Pennsylvania. I was on a full expense account and I pretty much banked my entire paycheck. I was like the drunken sailor who had a girl in every port. Life was good and I was enjoying it.

On my scheduled travels to Oakland, CA., I would stay with friends who I had known since 1960. I found out that on one of their relocations through Brockway, they had purchased a house owned by a dentist and his wife. I didn't know them but remember them telling the tragic story that the dentist had leukemia and was not expected to live.

Prior to my starting the Management Training Program, the dentist passed away. I remember riding to work and looking at the house they were building on top of Mt. Vista. My friends told me the sad story. She was widowed in an unfinished home with four small children under the age of nine. Everyone told me the house was pretty well finished except for hanging a few light fixtures and mounting some switch plates. As I was to find out later, this was far from the truth.

Since I was considered to be an eligible bachelor around Brockway, people were always trying "to fix me up." My California friends were no different. When

I would visit them in Oakland they would tell me about the "Widow on the Hill" and suggested I take her out on a date. They thought that she was a very nice girl and we would hit it off. I told them I would take her out but was privately thinking, "Why do I want to take out a widow with four children in an unfinished house?" Unbeknownst to me, my friends had been writing to the widow and telling her all about me.

In fact, I had no intention of taking her out.

In March of 1970, I was making my last swing through California and told my mother, father and sister, Kris, that I would take them along and we would have a family vacation in California. None of my family had ever been to California. While we were in Oakland, my mother, father, Kris and I stayed with my friends and they would bend my mother's ear and tell her about the sad situation of the dentist and his wife, Carole.

It was in California that we first noticed my father was having health problems. As we were walking up to Coit Tower in San Francisco, he experienced shortness of breath and we had to stop several times for him to rest. Later, I was so thankful we had taken the California vacation since we had such a good time and it was to be the last time we were together as a family.

A short time after we returned home to DuBois, PA. my father experienced chest pains and shortness of breath. He went into the hospital and while there suffered a massive heart attack that destroyed a major portion of his heart. They moved him into Intensive Care so they could keep a better eye on him. He was very critical for several days.

I HAVE ALWAYS BELIEVED THERE IS GOOD IN EVERY BAD. JAC BEIGHEY'S ILLINESS WAS TO DRAMATICALLY AND SIGNIFICENTLY CHANGE MY LIFE FOREVER.

I would sit in the Intensive Care Waiting Room for hours every day watching my father. My mother was always there too. We were only allowed into ICU for five minutes every hour, so it was very difficult to get information on how my father was doing.

THE BEST DAY OF MY LIFE came while I was sitting in the waiting room. I noticed a cute nurse who was working in ICU. My testosterone started to kick in. She looked so adorable in her nursing uniform … A cute smile with her tongue rolled up in the corner. I thought, "I have got to find out who that is." I got close enough to see her name tag … Carole Lanzoni. I thought, "Oh my God, that's the girl I was supposed to be taking out all this time." I was pretty embarrassed and went into hiding.

Whenever the ICU nurses would go on a break, my mother would follow them into the coffee shop and pump them for information about my father's condition. I found out later that on one occasion, my mother followed Carole into the coffee shop and started a conversation with her. During the conversation, Carole mentioned about her husband, a dentist, dying of leukemia in Brockway. My mother remembered the story from the visit to Oakland, California and said, "Do you have friends in Oakland, California?"

I was sitting in the waiting room reading a book when suddenly my mother appeared with Carole Lanzoni and said, "You have mutual friends in Oakland, California." I was very embarrassed. I hid it the best that I could.

From that moment on, I saw or talked to Carole Lanzoni almost every single day. We were married eight months later.

Fortunately, my father lived long enough to see us get married and to meet Carole, Skip, Susie, Tom and Tim. I always felt sad that he never got to see or know our two youngest children, Elizabeth and Anne.

WHAT STARTED OUT AS A SAD TIME IN MY LIFE HAD A HAPPY ENDING! I MARRIED THE GIRL OF MY DREAMS WHO HAS BEEN A GREAT AND SUPPORTIVE WIFE AND MOTHER FOR OVER 35 YEARS.

YES, THERE IS GOOD IN EVERY BAD.

Have a Vision

To me, it was always a big help in a new business situation to understand the vision, goals and objectives necessary to accomplish your mission.

These same principles apply in your personal and family life. Family mission statements, or visions, are a way of transferring your highly effective business habits to your home life.

Your family and/or personal vision are the "big picture" of what you want to be. They display your beliefs and values. They are succinct and personal.

I have written a family and personal mission and the goals and objectives to accomplish them.

Writing down our values has led us to talk more about what we want out of our marriage, our family and our lives. I have them prominently displayed in our homes and have had them framed for each of our children.

Goals are lofty ideals that you continue to strive for but may never reach. I continue to reach for my goals every day – sometimes with little or no success – but the next day I pick myself up and start all over again.

Objectives are the specific things that are necessary to accomplish if you are going to reach your goals.

Having a vision has been a roadmap for success in my life. I have included it here for your perusal ... I pray that in some small way it may be a positive influence in your life.

BEIGHEY FAMILY MISSION STATEMENT

TO CREATE A NURTURING PLACE OF FAITH, ORDER, TRUTH, LOVE, HAPPINESS AND RELAXATION; AND, TO PROVIDE OPPORTUNITY FOR EACH PERSON TO BECOME RESPONSIBLY INDEPENDENT AND EFFECTIVELY INTERDEPENDENT IN ORDER TO SERVE WORTHY PURPOSES IN SOCIETY

LARRY BEIGHEY MISSION STATEMENT

WITH INTEGRITY, BE PROACTIVE AND VALUE-DRIVEN IN PHYSICAL, SPIRITUAL, EMOTIONAL AND INTELLECTUAL INTERACTIONS IN PERSONAL, FAMILY, BUSINESS AND SOCIAL RELATIONSHIPS

GOALS

PHYSICAL
REACH AND MAINTAIN THE PROPER LEVEL OF BODY WEIGHT AND AEROBIC WELL-BEING FOR MY AGE AND HEIGHT

SPIRITUAL
PRACTICE, TEACH AND BELIEVE IN THE HOLY TRINITY – FATHER, SON AND HOLY GHOST

EMOTIONAL
CONTROL EMOTIONS … BE PATIENT … REDUCE STRESS

INTELLECTUAL
CONTINUOUSLY EXPAND MY INTELLECTUAL KNOWLEDGE

If You Haven't Touched It in Two Years - Throw It Out

I don't care if it is old papers, computer files, a filing cabinet, or kitchen pots and pans – if you haven't used it for two years, get rid of it.

It is almost a 100% probability or "a sure thing" that if you haven't referred to or used something for a period of two years, you are probably never going to need it again.

Why two years? There is nothing magical about two years … make it one year or three years, but do it.

Now you are probably saying to yourself, "What if I need it and now it's gone?" The very few times that this may happen to you will be far outweighed by the reduction in your clutter and your peace of mind.

I have always prided myself on being a very organized person, but I still find that I must discipline myself to periodically go through all of my possessions and purge all the unnecessary information, papers and other things that I let myself accumulate. You should do the same … it will make your life a lot easier.

It's History ... Learn from It

If you read a lot of history books, you will find out that some of the great generals and politicians have constantly read history as a basis for planning their future strategies. It is no different in your everyday walks of life ... you will continue to use history or past experiences to determine how you will face day-to-day problems.

When you stop to think about it, history, past experiences and precedents are used in many disciplines, including perhaps the greatest of all: the common law court systems used in the United States.

I have found that using historical experiences in my everyday life has proved to be one of the most effective tools in making good decisions.

Why "reinvent the wheel" if you can use past experiences to guide you in making sound decisions? "It's history ... learn from it."

21

Just Like Streetcars: One Goes
By Every Five Minutes

Well, this is another gem that is attributable to my father, Jac Beighey. I had just graduated from college and entered the business world as an Industrial Engineer. I had never owned an automobile of my own and was in the market to purchase my first car. I had "the fever" and wanted to buy a car real fast. Our neighbor had a beautiful white Oldsmobile convertible that was only a couple of years old and he wanted to sell it. I loved the car and wanted to buy it in the worst kind of way, but thought it would be best if I talked it over with my father to get his advice.

As was typical of my father, he pointed out all the options and the pros and cons of buying a used car or buying a new car. I remember being disgusted with the conversation and just wanting to buy the used car. He sensed my frustration and then uttered the famous saying, "They're just like streetcars, one goes by about every five minutes."

He then proceeded to tell me that it wasn't the only car in the world; that there would be many others; and, that I should take my time and really think it out.

Of course, he was right. A few weeks later, with his help, I bought my first car – a brand-new Chevy convertible the day that the new models were released. I loved that car!

It was a lesson well learned and one I have tried to pass along to my children and business associates. Don't be hasty in your decisions. "They're just like streetcars: one goes by about every five minutes."

Keep a Calendar

As I mentioned before, I am a very organized person and have tried to pass the same traits on to my family and colleagues.

My wife is a remarkable person, but I don't think she could have run the house and raised six beautiful children without her calendar.

My family has always kidded me about not going anywhere without my "purse," an 8 1/2 x 11" leather, zippered, 3-ring briefcase that I always have with me. It is my Bible and I am lost without it.

In my "purse," I keep a calendar, contacts and important notes about my goals, objectives, projects and other important information as well as my personal notes on various subjects.

I keep all the information on my computer with an organizer software database and print it out about once a year to put in my "purse." I keep the notebook up to date by writing new events and contacts in it and transferring them to my "purse" on an as-needed basis so both my computer and notebook have the same information. I now have over 700 contacts in my files and I can sort and print them out in many different ways.

Today, many people use handheld PDA organizers and this may be the way to go; but I still like to use the 8 1/2 x 11" notebook, because you can take any correspondence, three-hole punch it and put it in your notebook.

It's Easier to Get Forgiveness than It Is to Get Permission

So many times in your life you run into situations where you ask if you can do something and you are told 'no' ... many times without even a chance to argue your case. Or other times you are told to do something that you don't want to do.

One of my most vivid memories of this was attending a bankruptcy auction in New York City. At issue was a manufacturing line that made ammunition boxes for the United States Army. We already had a line in our company, which generated a high profit, but this different size would make a very good addition.

In this case, my superiors gave me a "threshold" and a "ceiling" price that I was not to exceed without checking back with them.

During the auction, the price quickly went to my "ceiling" and there wasn't time to check in with my superiors. I made a spontaneous and unilateral decision to go over the "ceiling." We were successful in securing the ammunition line and it generated a high level of profit for many years and I "got forgiveness."

It is my observation that people generally make the same decision as someone else would in the same situation and even though they won't give you permission, they will give you forgiveness. This is not always the case, and you must think it through very carefully before you take such an action.

I am not advocating that you should pursue a radical or dangerous approach in your actions, but sometimes it might be worthwhile to follow your ideas.

I am suggesting this approach should be followed only after the situation has been thoroughly analyzed and all the ramifications investigated; then you will find that it is easier to get forgiveness than it is to get permission.

24

Life Is a Contact Sport

Although it doesn't seem fair, sometimes it is true that as you go through life, "it is who you know, not what you know." Be that as it may, it does not minimize the importance of making and keeping good contacts.

It has been proven that over 80% of the people searching for a new job find that position through contacts they have made. It does not come from resumes, mailing letters, search firms or other means.

It is true that having contacts alone will not get you through life, but it does open doors for you that would otherwise be closed; and, many times it will put your name in front of someone that otherwise would not have encountered it.

I have found through the years that it is always important to keep a complete contact list.

I keep all of my contacts in an Organizer file that now has over 700 names, categorized in many different ways so I can search for the person or discipline that

I am looking for. Once a year I go through my contact list and "weed out" obsolete contacts. Surprisingly, when I finish this process, I still end up with about 700 names.

25

Make Something Happen

Many years ago, I was coaching a baseball team in a 13-15 year old league. I kept telling the players that they could not always just play the game, but that sometimes you had to do whatever it takes to "make something happen."

In one game, we were losing in the late innings and I implored the batter to "make something happen." We had runners in scoring position with two out, but the batter hit a routine ground ball to the shortstop and I thought the inning would be over. The runner was going to be out by a couple of strides. Surprise! He slid into first base, startling the first baseman. He dropped the ball. The runner was safe and we won the game.

This was about a baseball game, but it works in all aspects of life: Make something happen.

Surround Yourself with Good People

"You get pushed up from the bottom, not pulled up from the top." This certainly seems like it is true so it is very important to "surround yourself with good people."

It has been said that you are only as good as the people around you. A prime example is the case comparison between Richard Nixon and Ronald Reagan.

Richard Nixon chose to surround himself with an arrogant, manipulative, scheming staff that controlled virtually all access to the President. Let's look what happened to them:

- John Mitchell – former Attorney General
- H. R Haldeman – White House Chief of staff
- John Erlichman – Assistant to Nixon for Domestic Affairs

These men were all convicted of conspiracy and obstruction of justice and served many years in prison. President Nixon resigned in disgrace

Compare Nixon's men to the people around President Reagan:

- George Schultz – Chairman of Bechtel Corporation, one of the largest construction companies in the world
- James Baker – A lawyer who has served four Presidents and has received the Presidential Medal of Freedom
- Donald Regan – Former Chairman of Merrill Lynch

I think you can readily see the difference and know which group of people you would want to surround yourself with … I know which group I would want advising me.

It is very important to surround yourself with good, capable people: You are only as good as the people around you.

4 F

Freedom, Faith, Friends and Family! These are my 4 F's.

I first heard President George H. W. Bush (Bush 41) talk about them at a motivational seminar in Atlanta, Georgia shortly after he left office in the early nineties. I adopted the 4 F's and use them to help guide me.

FREEDOM
In our hectic, day-to-day lives we seldom if ever take the time to think about and give thanks for our freedom. As I am writing this we are engaged in "The War on Terrorism." The terrorists want to deny us our freedoms just like they did on 9/11. I don't think we want to give up our hard earned sovereignty like women's rights, voting, free expression and freedom of speech. It is a battle we must endure and win ... "Don't tread on us."

FAITH
I feel it is so important to have faith in some higher level being. You must have beliefs and convictions to help get through our day-to-day lives. Isn't it great that

we have freedom of religion to be able to openly pray and meditate for our personal guidance.

FRIENDS
I have always said that you can count yourself lucky if you have more friends than you can count on one hand. I am talking about "Best Man" type of friends. These are the friends that will be there for you no matter what ... a friend you can talk to for advice and counseling in strictest confidence ... a friend that will help you financially if you find yourself in great need ... a friend that will tell you straight even though it may affect your friendship.

I count myself lucky that I had four such friends. Unfortunately, I have lost three of them at early ages and the fourth was in a terrible automobile accident that left him less than 100%. He, too, recently died. My friends were there for me when I needed them and I think I served them well when they needed me.

FAMILY
The last F is for family. I saved it for last because I feel it is so important. When things are at a low level and you are most in need you can always turn to your family unit. We have always told our children that no one loves you like your spouse and your family. You can always count on your kin in a time of need.

As I have mentioned, it pleases my wife and I that our children's best friends are their brothers and sisters. It makes us happy that our immediate and extended families are so close and caring for each other. Our door is always open to our family group as their doors are always open to us.

28

NIH

Now this is a funny name. "NIH" stands for Not Invented Here. How many times have you told someone about an idea and they just rejected it out of hand because of "NIH" ... Not Invented Here? People have a tendency to disregard a new idea that is not theirs. I don't know the reason, but it's a very common occurrence in a social or business environment.

Socially, people are always resistant to someone else's ideas. How many times have you heard somebody say that they went to the greatest restaurant the other night? Well that's because they found it. If we said we found the best restaurant the other night, they may say, they tried that before and it was just OK. That's because it's not their discovery ... Not Invented Here ... "NIH."

In a business environment, people are always trying ideas on their boss, but many times it is rejected out of hand because it was not the boss's idea. Some time later the boss will bring up the same issue and "run with it" ... now it's his idea.

It is unclear why people are so susceptible to "NIH" ... Not Invented Here. It may be from fear; it may be from jealousy; it may be from competitive edge – but whatever the reason, its "NIH" ... Not Invented Here.

The best way to deal with "NIH" is to "Plant a Seed." Then, if you can make someone else think it is there idea, you have a much greater chance it will be accepted.

If You Build It, They Will Come

Serving as my company's Energy Czar during the 1970's energy crisis, I gained some extensive experience in the energy field. In my opinion, during that period, the consumer got caught up in a battle between the government and the energy companies. They said there was a shortage of fossil fuels; but, surprisingly, when the price of oil got high enough, there was no longer a shortage.

There are several long-term energy areas – such as solar, wind, corn alcohol, etc. – that are research-intensive and expensive but give promise as long-term solutions.

For years, I have felt that there was some middle ground for energy growth. These would include drilling in the ANWR fields of Alaska and off the coast of Florida. But in my opinion, the one that has the greatest potential is nuclear power.

Only 20% of the U.S. energy supply is nuclear and there have not been any new plants put in operation since

1979 – over twenty-five years ago. In fact, a nuclear power plant has been built in the Northeastern area of the United States and has NEVER been turned on.

Are there dangers? Of course ... but don't the rewards far outweigh the risks?

Worldwide, as of May 2005, there are 439 nuclear energy reactors in operation and 137 under construction, planned or proposed. Of the 137, NONE are in the United States.

So where are they?

France: 78% of the French energy supply is nuclear, with 59 reactors in operation.

China: 15 reactors operational with 31 in the works.

Russia: 17 nuclear reactors operating, generating 17% of Russian energy usage; they have another 13 underway or planned.

Japan: 25% of their power is generated from 54 operating reactors, and they have another 14 in their future.

South Korea: 20 nuclear generation plants producing 40% of their requirements; another 8 planned.

England and Canada: These two nations have more reactors per capita than the U.S., with 40 plants in operation and 5 under construction or planned.

What do these countries know that we in the U.S. don't?

With the right regulations and controls, nuclear power can be our shortest path to achieving a self-sufficient energy level that will greatly reduce our dependency on imported oil.

Surprisingly, decreasing our dependence on foreign oil will increase the oil supply and decrease the price of the imported oil ... The Arab sheiks need the money ... Supply and Demand wins again.

Plan, Organize, Control

One of the most interesting jobs I ever had was teaching management principles to front-line supervisors in each of my company's 13 plants. It required me to have a thorough understanding of management while allowing me to get to know every supervisor in every plant. Over the years, I have passed these principles, along with my thoughts and observations, on to my family.

<u>Management</u>

Management is defined as the setting and accomplishing of objectives through the planning, organizing and control of human and physical resources. Further, control is broken down into delegation and follow-up.

It is important – in fact, imperative – that all three functions (planning, organizing and control) be followed. Frequently, one or more of these functions is overlooked or merely given "lip service."

A must-read book on these subjects is *The Seven Habits of Highly Effective People* by Steven Covey.

I recommend that all people read this book or listen to the audio book.

Planning

A good plan should have three or four lofty goals that you strive to accomplish. Some possible goals might be:

- Meet financial objectives
- Provide a healthy home
- Provide a good quality of life for all family members

In "Have a Vision," I shared with you my personal vision or mission and showed you my personal goals … one each in the spiritual, intellectual, physical and emotional areas.

Notice that these goals are general and lofty but contain no specific, measurable objectives. You must write measurable objectives that, when accomplished, will help you to reach your goals.

Organization

Any group must be organized if you are going to meet your objectives and reach your goals.

Everyone cannot be allowed to "do their own thing." There must be a chain of command.

Control

Finally, the organization must function effectively if the plans are going to be accomplished. To do this you must control the organization or unit. This is the important 3rd phase-control, which is broken down into delegation and follow-up.

Delegation

It is better to build a plan from the bottom-up than the top-down. Having everyone involved in the planning will ensure that everyone "buys into" the process.

It should be true that, if the objectives are accomplished, then the strategies and goals should be obtained as long as there are no external factors.

After the first management function – planning – has been developed by the group and delegated to the rest of the organization, how is the final step – control – accomplished?

Follow-up

It is common to see a good plan, organization and/ or delegation fail because there was no follow-up. Too often, the approach is to delegate a project to an individual and then walk away from it.

This is a much-overlooked part of management and is the main reason that plans are not accomplished.

Pushed Up from Bottom, Not Pulled Up from Top

Why is it that some people always seem to get ahead of other people who appear to be more on the ball or have more to offer?

Many people feel that, if they "suck up" to their boss or other important individuals, they will move up the social or business ladder.

In fact, just the opposite is true. The more support you have from your peers or subordinates, the more likely you are to be a success.

I remember a story about a man who was a department head in a factory. He did a good job and had the respect of all the people who worked for and with him. His superiors recognized that he was doing a good job; so, when another department was in trouble, they asked him to take over the responsibility of that department. Again, he earned the respect of all the people around him; so, his superiors gave him another department to supervise and manage. Before anybody realized it, he was soon the manager of almost all the departments in the factory. His superiors decided they might as well make him the plant manager since he was already running most of the departments.

The moral of the story is that, if you want to get ahead in your personal or professional careers, you must earn the respect, admiration and dedication from those working around you. In the end, it is through their efforts that you'll become successful. You will be "pushed up from the bottom, not pulled up from the top."

Remember Names

One of the most useful and successful techniques in getting along with people is to remember their names.

Early in my business career, I learned a useful technique that helped me gain the respect of my personal and business acquaintances.

I traveled extensively, visiting the many sales offices and manufacturing plants of my company. The visits would be of a short duration, but I would visit each site frequently.

I decided to build a logbook for each location by writing down the names of each individual. I would try to remember each person's name and other tidbits of information about them such as their wife's name, birthdays, children's names and other interesting facts about them. As soon as I left them, I would jot down as many names and facts as I could remember. Later, when I was alone, I would enter my notes into my logbook.

When it was time to visit each location, I would pull out my logbook and browse through the names and facts. Many times I could not remember who the people were or what they looked like, but when I saw them it immediately came back to me. I would walk up to them and say, "Hi, Bob, how are you doing today? How is Mary? Is Mike still playing Little League baseball?" They would remark, "How do you remember all that?"

Sometimes I wouldn't see an individual for over a year, but by just reviewing my logbook of names before I arrived, I could recall many facts.

I have used this technique since the early 1960s and found it to be very successful. Everyone likes to hear their name and talk about their life and family. By mentioning their name or by asking a simple question, people will feel a close relationship with you and you will have earned their respect and admiration.

Set Goals

Goals are broad, general statements and do not include numbers, times, cost or any other measurable parameter.

Strategies provide further refinement on how to accomplish each goal. Strategies are not measurable and there are usually less than half a dozen (6) for each goal.

Under each strategy are the objectives that specifically detail what is to be accomplished.

Again, objectives must be specific and measurable.

However, the area needing the most attention is action plans. This area, under measurable objectives, tells specifically, how to accomplish the objective.

As a guide, I have repeated my Personal Mission Statement here along with my goals and objectives.

LARRY BEIGHEY MISSION STATEMENT

WITH INTEGRITY, BE PROACTIVE AND VALUE DRIVEN IN PHYSICAL, SPIRITUAL, EMOTIONAL AND INTELLECTUAL INTERACTIONS IN PERSONAL, FAMILY AND SOCIAL RELATIONSHIPS

<u>PHYSICAL GOAL</u>

REACH AND MAINTAIN THE PROPER LEVEL OF BODY WEIGHT AND AEROBIC WELL-BEING FOR MY AGE AND HEIGHT

<u>OBJECTIVES</u>
ACHIEVE THIRTY-TWO COOPER AEROBIC POINTS PER WEEK

LOSE TWO POUNDS PER WEEK UNTIL I REACH MY IDEAL WEIGHT OF TWO HUNDRED POUNDS; THEN, MAINTAIN MY IDEAL BODY WEIGHT

DRINK EIGHT, EIGHT-OUNCE GLASSES OF WATER PER DAY

DRINK ONLY DECAFFEINATED COFFEE OR LIMIT REGULAR COFFEE TO TWO CUPS PER DAY

BRUSH AND FLOSS TEETH EVERY MORNING AND EVERY EVENING

HAVE AN ANNUAL PHYSICAL IN FIRST
QUARTER EVERY YEAR

HAVE TEETH CLEANED AND CHECKED TWICE
PER YEAR

FOLLOW A FIFTEEN HUNDRED CALORE-A-DAY
LOW FAT/LOW CARBOHYDRATE EXCHANGE
DIET

SPIRITUAL GOAL

PRACTICE, TEACH, AND BELIEVE IN THE HOLY
TRINITY – FATHER …. SON …. HOLY GHOST

OBJECTIVES
ATTEND CHURCH AT LEAST THREE TIMES
PER WEEK

READ THREE CHAPTERS OF THE BIBLE EACH
WEEK

ENJOY FIFTEEN MINUTES OF MEDITATION
AND PRAYER EVERY DAY

EMOTIONAL GOAL

CONTROL EMOTIONS … BE PATIENT … REDUCE STRESS

OBJECTIVES

LISTEN BEFORE SPEAKING …. THEN GET FEEDBACK BY REPEATING WHAT YOU HEARD

ONLY SAY POSITIVE THINGS

APOLOGIZE TO EACH INDIVIDUAL EVERY TIME YOU LOSE YOUR TEMPER WITH THEM

KISS CAROLE EVERY DAY AND TELL HER I LOVE HER

SPEND ONE HOUR PER DAY OF QUALITY TIME WITH CAROLE

ENJOY TWENTY HOURS PER WEEK OF RECREATION TIME (GOLF, PIANO, MOVIES, PLAYS AND PROJECTS)

INTELLECTUAL GOAL

CONTINUOUSLY EXPAND MY INTELLECTUAL KNOWLEDGE

OBJECTIVES

LIMIT TV WATCHING TO FIFTEEN HOURS PER WEEK

READ TWO BOOKS PER MONTH

READ ONE NEWSPAPER PER WEEK

READ ONE NEWSLETTER OR NEWS MAGAZINE
PER WEEK

DEVELOP COMPUTER PROFICIENCY IN WORD,
QUICKEN, AMERICA ON-LINE, AND LOTUS
ORGANIZER

34

Roots and Wings

Raising six children (a "Brady Bunch" – three boys and three girls) is a daunting task. We always tried to provide deep "roots" for our children; but, we also tried to instill in them the "wings" to fly away on their own.

As our Family Mission Statement says, we tried "TO CREATE A NURTURING PLACE OF FAITH, ORDER, TRUTH, LOVE, HAPPINESS AND RELAXATION; AND, TO PROVIDE OPPORTUNITY FOR EACH PERSON TO BECOME RESPONSIBLY INDEPENDENT AND EFFECTIVELY INTERDEPENDENT IN ORDER TO SERVE WORTHY PURPOSES IN SOCIETY."

As I write this, our six children range in age from 31 to 47 ... hardly children anymore. Some are married, some are not ... some have children; some do not ... most importantly, all are good people. All of them have "wings" and have "flown the nest;" but, one of the things that makes us the happiest is that their brothers and sisters are their best friends. In fact, each year, they vacation together and once a year the three girls get together for "Sisters' Weekend" without their spouses or children.

One of the things I witnessed along this journey was the negative effect working in the same business as their father could present on their lives.

I observed several situations where this was true.

No matter how good a job the individual does (they are probably quite capable of doing a superior job), someone is always going to say, "They only got there because of their father." Even though the individual is capable of achieving this level on their own, there will always be this "black cloud" hanging over them, which can shape their self-confidence.

The potential problem manifests itself even more if it is a private business. Here the additional danger is retirement. Unless the senior member has provided for some retirement package, I am afraid they will "die with their boots on."

When we bought our own company, my 50-50 partner and I talked about this and made the decision that we would not have family members working "in the business." We both felt that our children were quite capable of achieving a high level of success on their own. Five years later, we sold the company for enough money so that eventually, they will be handsomely rewarded; and, during our "twilight years" we will enjoy a great "quality of life."

Roots and wings ... think about it.

1

The Mayonnaise Jar

When things in your life seem almost too much to handle, when 24 hours in a day are not enough, remember the story about the mayonnaise jar.

A professor stood before his philosophy class and had some items in front of him. When the class began, wordlessly, he picked up a very large, empty mayonnaise jar and proceeded to fill it with golf balls. He then asked the students if the jar was full. They agreed that it was.

So the professor then picked up a box of pebbles and poured them into the jar. He shook the jar lightly. The pebbles rolled into the open areas between the golf balls. He then asked the students again if the jar was full. They agreed that it was.

The professor next picked up a box of sand and poured it into the jar. Of course, the sand filled up everything else. He asked once more if the jar was full. The students responded with a unanimous "yes." The professor then produced two glasses of water from under the table and poured the entire contents into the jar, effectively filling the empty space between the sand. Then he stuck a bouquet of flowers in the jar.

"Now," said the professor, "I want you to recognize that this jar represents your life. The golf balls are the important things – your family, your children, your health, your friends, your favorite passions – things that if everything else was lost and only they remained, your life would still be full."

"The pebbles are the other things that matter, like your job, your house, your car."

"The sand is everything else – the small stuff. If you put the sand into the jar first," he continued, "there is no room for the pebbles or the golf balls. The same goes for life. If you spend all your time and energy on the small stuff, you will never have room for the things that are important to you."

"Pay attention to the things that are critical to your happiness. Play with your children. Take time to get medical checkups. Take your partner out to dinner. Play another 18. There will always be time to clean the house and fix the disposal. Take care of the golf balls first, the things that really matter. Set your priorities. The rest is just sand."

One of the students raised their hand and inquired what the water and flowers represented. The professor smiled. "I'm glad you asked. It just goes to show you that no matter how full your life may seem there's always time to "Smell the Flowers.""

Strategic Planning

The more I study successful people, families, organizations and companies, I find that the common thread that runs through it all is a well thought-out and documented mission statement and strategic planning.

Business strategic planning played a big role in the success of each of the companies I worked for.

Strategic planning was the basis for Newt Gingrich's plan, in 1982, to take over the majority and become Speaker of the House by 1996. He achieved it two years early.

I knew *The Seven Habits of Highly Effective People* by Stephen Covey had been on the Best Seller List for a long time and is on Newt Gingrich's Required Reading List, so I thought I should read it.

I found the book to be very effective to individual and family career planning and urge you to read it.

After reading the book, I wrote my Personal Strategic Plan and enclosed a copy in the "Set Goals" *Drop* as a guide to what a Personal Strategic Plan may look like. Remember, this is a dynamic document and should be reviewed and revised many times during your lifetime as your situation changes. Although my goals were in the area of physical, intellectual, emotional and spiritual, some other areas might include financial, career, social and family.

As you may know, a strategic plan contains:

- A mission statement
- Situation analysis–internal and external
- Strengths and weaknesses
- Goals – general
- Strategies – generally how to reach goals
- Operational plans or Objectives – specific

I was always advised to only have three to four goals at any time. Remember, goals are something lofty that you reach for but may never obtain. Strategies are how you are going to reach your goals; and, operational plans are specific and measurable objectives that must be accomplished in order to fulfill your strategies and reach your goals. As a rule, goals and strategies should not contain numbers or time deadlines. However, it is important to remember that the format is not as important as getting your strategic plan down on paper, regardless of your age.

I recommend that every family and/or individual have a "Strategic Plan."

Capital Gains

I think I understand the taxation on Capital Gains and Corporate Dividends. It is double taxation. The Federal Income Tax code taxes a corporation's profits at the Corporate Tax Rate before any dividends are paid. When the corporation pays dividends to its stockholders, the stockholders dividends are again taxed. This is double taxation.

It is true that the elimination of the dividend tax would benefit the wealthiest taxpayers. However, a recent article in the *USA Today* newspaper indicates that 52 percent of the households paying taxes now own corporate stocks; so, the elimination of the tax on taxpayers' dividends would decrease the taxes and increase the disposable income for a majority of the taxpayers. The wealthiest taxpayers will receive a much greater reduction in their income tax than a middle class taxpayer.

What I don't understand and don't see mentioned in any news broadcast or newspaper article is what the wealthiest taxpayers would do with the reduction in income tax they receive from the elimination of the taxation on dividends. What will they do with the increase in disposable income they receive?

It only makes sense that one of two things will happen with the increase in disposable income that taxpayers have realized:

- Taxpayers will spend the additional disposal income to buy goods and services from stores and companies. This rise in demand should increase the sales and profit of companies, hopefully generating additional capital investment and creating jobs.
- If the taxpayers do not spend the additional disposable income on goods and services, they are certainly not going to "hide the money under the mattress." They will reinvest the increased disposable income in stocks, bonds and/or CD's, creating more investment dollars for corporations producing goods and services or for banks to loan to individuals.

In both cases, the money supply for goods and services in corporations and banks is going to increase, allowing them to increase capital investments and/or loans, creating more jobs and increasing the company's profits, allowing them to increase dividends.

It has been proven that this type of "trickle-down" economics will stimulate the economy by creating more capital investment, which will increase wages and jobs, thus improving individuals' disposable and/ or investment income.

As Ronald Reagan stated so eloquently, "The government does not create jobs and improve the economy by higher taxation. It is private enterprise, through capital investment, that increases corporate profits and increases jobs and individuals' disposable income having the greatest impact on the economy." (See "Economic Growth.")

38

Compulsive Behavior

As I reach the "sunset years," I have become increasingly aware of the effect compulsive behavior has had on my family and friends.

I am certainly not a prude and did my share of drinking when I was "sowing my wild oats" and I kept it up until I got married. Fortunately, Carole and I steadily decreased our alcohol consumption to the point that we are now "social" drinkers. At no time did we drink at home by ourselves or allow our children to drink at home except for a small glass of wine or champagne on a holiday.

I had four really close friends in my life ... "Best Man" type of friends. Alcohol has taken three of them at ages 40, 59, and 65. One was a lawyer; one a CPA; one owned an insurance firm. All were married and two had children. Two ended up divorced and one ended up in a homeless shelter.

There are many other forms of compulsive behavior besides alcohol ... gambling, drugs, stealing, and eating disorders ... and on and on and on.

I mention this to point out that compulsive behavior picks on all types and has a devastating affect on individuals and their families and friends. No amount of talking, financial support or intervention by family or friends helped these individuals.

It is important to watch for signs of compulsive behavior and give these individuals love, support and help to fight their obsessive actions.

39

Economic Growth

I am writing this *Drop in the Bucket* on June 7, 2004, as we are remembering the passing of one of our greatest presidents, Ronald Reagan.

I was very impressed with a quote that Ronald Reagan made that I have not yet seen on the TV or newspapers as they remember Reagan with wall-to-wall coverage of his legacy. I was so moved by the message that I had it blown up and framed … it hung in our company conference room for many years during the 90's and now hangs in my private office.

To me, Reagan captured the difference between the government and the private sector in one concise paragraph – it speaks for itself and I will include it here as it was said and printed.

"Economic growth is created by people who produce things. The more that's produced to meet increasing demand, the more new jobs and services are created in turn. Other than short-term make-work projects, the

government does not create jobs; the private sector does. How? By investing in new plants and equipment, and by researching and developing new products. And how does the private sector do all that? By having enough corporate profits to reinvest and enough incentives to make such expenditures desirable."

I think he got it right ... how about you?

Make Notes

I have always told the people around me to write things down and not rely on their memory. Some people have great minds and memories, but even they forget things.

I was fortunate to be part of an organization that also believed in keeping notes and writing things down. They used a formal Time Management System so that everyone was on the same system. They held seminars for all the management people, teaching them how to organize their time and manage their notes and filing. It was a very simple system and I picked up on it quickly.

One of the interesting things that we were taught was to organize items and notes by people's name, rather than subject matter or date. It is easier to remember who told you something than try to remember what they said or when they said it. Try it … you will be surprised. It works.

As I mentioned in "Keep a Calendar," the 8 ½ x 11" system always started with a calendar, followed by Projects and Personal Notes. 8 ½ x 11" is a great size to 3-hole punch papers and letters and save them in the notebook.

Another important thing to remember is to date and initial your work. You will be surprised how many times you will find that date to be important and help you out of many situations.

I have tried to instill these same practices into my family with what I think has been great success. Some of them use a very formal outline system with their own version of shorthand. Some do it electronically. Others have notes all over the page … but they all keep a calendar and notes.

41

Shake Hands

The glass container plant that I managed had over 1000 employees and ran 24 hours a day, 7 days a week.

I had been there about seven or eight months when the Christmas/New Year period approached. I thought I should find some way to say "thank you," but it was very difficult since so many people worked on different shifts and it was a large plant covering acres of land. Fortunately, everyone had to funnel through one time clock (a practice I didn't like … punching a time clock was demeaning … as hard as I tried I never got rid of the time clock; but, that is another subject.)

At the end of each shift, I positioned myself at the time clock and as each employee came by I shook their hand and thanked them for the job they had done for the company and for me.

I got all kinds of favorable reactions, including some women trying to kiss me. I was much younger then. I joked that my wife was very jealous and would "deck me" if I went home with lipstick on my face.

The most poignant and memorable experience was the woman who had walked all the way out to the parking lot in the ice and snow, then turned around and walked back in. She approached me and said, "I have been working here for over 25 years and no one has ever thanked me for the job I have done." She gave me a quick peck on the cheek and said, "Thank you."

Take Counsel

One of the things that you learn as you go through life is that you don't know everything … that is why it is so important to "take counsel."

I know many people that do not take advice very well. You know the stock answers: "That will never work;" "We tried that; it didn't work;" "You don't understand;" and, "We are going to do it our way."

I never understood this kind of reaction. I have always tried to teach people and my family to "take counsel." Listen to the opinions of as many other people as you can, especially those people who have lots of knowledge and education on the subject at hand.

You can sort through all the advice and counsel but in the end you make the decision. So, what do you have to lose except a little time?

Remember "take counsel."

Meditation

In the mid-80s, I had a series of jobs that required me to affect the lives of a great many people – I guess you could have called me a "hatchet man." I admit it made a big impact on me since I was causing great pain to many families at various stages in their lives … I looked for some solace to help me get through it.

I would consider myself a man of some religious belief. I started attending a daily 7AM service at a local church. I could attend the service and still make it to work on time even though, at some point, it was a 35-minute drive. I went every weekday morning that I was in town.

When I started going to the church, there were probably five or six other businessmen there and we were relegated to the "cry room," a small, glassed-in room looking out onto the main sanctuary. Shortly thereafter, a new Pastor – an organized, witty, little Irishman in his 70's - came into the church and the number of attendees grew to the point that we had to move into the main sanctuary.

I watched the daily attendance continue to rise until there were over 100 businessmen attending the daily service.

Before I realized it, I had gone to church every weekday for over 10 years ... it made a big difference in my life. I found that these 20 minutes of daily meditation helped me get through the big decisions in my life and helped me deal with the effect I would have on other people's lives.

During this period, I found myself on the other end of the ladder when I lost my job ... I was 51, with two children in college.

I was fortunate to have found that these few minutes of thought, reflection and prayer each day helped me get through this difficult period and I recommend that all people find a few minutes for private meditation each day.

Rules Are Made for the Many Because of the Few

Unfortunately, this is so true. Many of the rules we had in the plant I managed were originally made for a few people, maybe only three or four out of one thousand. But everyone had to abide by the rules. This affected time clock control, vacation planning, sick leave, paid funeral leave and many other things.

One time, a female employee approached me and asked if she would get three days of paid funeral leave because her uncle had died. I informed her that aunts and uncles didn't qualify for paid funeral leave, but that I was very sorry and expressed my sympathy. I asked her if her uncle lived nearby, but she informed me that he lived in a neighboring state. I asked her if she was close to her uncle. She told me, "No, I never met him … I just wanted to see if I could get three days off with pay."

Another example was an employee whose father died in Italy … He only got three days off with pay.

It got so involved that we had detailed policies covering the deceased's relationship to the employee: "If an employee's funeral leave occurred on their regular day off, and on and on.

Because of the "rights" of a few, I was not allowed to use common sense and do what was right.

Because of the "rights" of a few, we are not allowed to put up a Christmas tree in many public places.

Because of the "rights" of a few, we are not allowed to say a prayer in a classroom or in the locker room before a high school athletic event.

Because of the "rights" of a few, we are not allowed to have the Ten Commandants – or any reference to God – posted in a non-secular building.

Remember, it was only 1954 when the words "under God" were added to the Pledge of Allegiance … now they want to take it out.

What are we going to change it to?

It is a sad commentary that in order to protect everyone's "rights," we have to make rules for the many because of the few.

45

Say Thank You

I have mentioned that I was the Plant Manager of a large factory in a small town, a place where everyone knew everyone else in the town. The plant had over a 1000 employees and had been there for over 40 years. It was the flagship plant since the company's corporate headquarters were located in the same town. The plant was under the microscope, and I felt the pressure since it was my first experience managing a group that large.

I was expected to spend a large amount of time in the factory and in fact, for the first year of my two-year stint, I was in the plant every day … that's right, 365 straight days.

I thought I should develop my own style of management and decided I would spend a lot of time out on the factory floor so I could "Stop, Look and Listen."

I walked by one machine operator at least four times a day. He was running a very fast and difficult baby food machine and he always turned out high-quality glass containers and was always on the job. I would pass him and we would nod at each other.

One day, after the same routine went on for several months, the light in my brain finally went on. I stopped and thanked him for the fine job he did for the company and for me. He told me that he appreciated my interest and praise. I developed a long, lasting friendship and he taught me a lot about making baby food containers and made suggestions that helped the whole plant and me.

How many times in your life have you taken the good things for granted and only focused on the problems?

Don't forget, no matter how big the problems, take the time to say "Thank You" for a job well done ... those two little words will pay you back many times over.

Year of Planned Action

Somewhere in my business career, I learned a simple technique that served me well in controlling my capital spending and accomplishing my goals and objectives. Over the years, I found that it also served me well in my domestic family life, and I passed it along to my children and their households. I believe it is a simple and powerful tool.

Every year, prepare a detailed budget of your income and expenses. Hopefully, you will have more income than expenses. If not, you will have to cut expenses or borrow money to get your budget to balance.

Let's assume that you have more income than expenses. This excess can be used for savings or capital spending such as furniture, cars, etc. This is where a Year of Planned Action really becomes helpful.

Start by making a list of all the "special" projects you would like to accomplish over the next several years. You can always change and revise this when necessary.

Next, estimate what each project will cost. A "ballpark" figure is good enough. Don't get bogged down in too much detail. As you will see later, your estimates will probably only affect one project down the list.

Place the list in prioritized order. This is easier than it seems. First, take a stab at putting them in the order that you think you would like to see them accomplished.

Once this is done, compare Project #1 to Project #2 ... If Project #2 is more important than Project #1, switch them. Then compare #2 to #3 ... Switch them if necessary. Then compare #3 to #4, and so on down the list. When you are done, you have them in prioritized order. Of course, you can redo the priority order at any time.

Now, go back to your budget and see how much excess money you have for your projects. Add up the cost estimates in your projects list until you reach this amount. Draw a line under this last project within the budget excess. These are the projects you can do over the next year.

If you want to do more, then you are going to have to find the money in some other place: cut spending, borrow, etc.

If you want to stay within the budget (something I would recommend), only plan on doing these projects. If you want to add another project to the list, THEN

YOU MUST CUT SOMETHING OF EQUAL VALUE
FROM ABOVE THE LINE.

Now you have "A Year of Planned Action," an easy tool
to help keep your spending in check. Try it … you will
find it simple and helpful.

Follow Your Dreams

My wife is a remarkable person. What she has accomplished at this point in her life makes any of my accomplishments pale in comparison.

Her first husband died the day after Christmas, leaving her with four children, ages two to nine. She was 30! Besides her own grief, she still had to cope with explaining the loss of their father to these four small children. They just couldn't understand what had happened to their father. When was he coming back?

While vacationing at her brother's lake cabin in Michigan's northern woods, she watched a mother raccoon and her babies feeding nightly at the stump outside the kitchen window. The idea came to write her stories through the eyes of animals, believing it would be less painful for children to relate to their loss.

Carole had a dream about writing but could never imagine how she would find the time, especially after marrying me and having two more children ... six children under the age of 11.

It was a great idea, but when would she ever find the time?

One Saturday afternoon, I told her that I was going to take the six kids out for about three or four hours and that she should do whatever she wanted.

When I returned home, I found that she had sat down at a typewriter (there were few personal computers in those days) and had written 30 pages of her book, *The Waddodles of Hollow Lake.* That was 31 years ago.

By sneaking a few minutes here or there – or staying up half the night after everyone had gone to bed – she typed away.

In 1986, we bought a personal computer and after a few quick lessons, Carole learned how to use a simple word processor. Soon, she was proficient in using the computer and had moved up to the most advanced word processors.

That was 1500 type-written pages ago.

She has now had two books published in the series, *The Waddodles of Hollow Lake,* and has written enough draft material for 5 or 6 books. (www.waddodles.com)

What started out as a dream has turned into a reality! It just proves the point that if you set your mind to something, you can find a way to get it accomplished, despite difficult odds and situations.

Remember to "follow your dreams" and as Theodore Waddodle, one of the raccoons in Carole's books says, "Always look forward, never behind."

48

Time Well Spent

When our six children were young and in their developmental years, we felt it was necessary to try to introduce a sense of duty and responsibly into their lives.

We tried all the "standard" techniques – including allowances, daily duties, family meetings and other ideas – with what we thought was limited success.

Our daughter, Susan Beighey Morrell, has taken it to a new level, developing a program called *Time Well Spent©*.

This program has been so successful that she has passed it on to numerous family members and individuals and has a copyright on the program.

Time Well Spent© teaches young people daily responsibilities with financial rewards. With her permission, I have included it here.

Time Well Spent©

As a wife and mother of four children ages 6-12, managing a household of six becomes increasingly challenging when piled on top of the everyday maintenance of the home. Each family member has his or her own diverse interests, school obligations, and social commitments. I found myself trying to find a way to manage the overwhelming bombardment of everyone's needs and wants and at the same time remain a happy mother and wife.

Over time, I developed a job chart system called *Time Well Spent©*. My system is simple to maintain, FUN, motivating, and individualized to each family member. I found the system slowly transfers the burden of managing everyone's daily tasks from my shoulders to the multiple shoulders of the family by assigning each task to the person who owns it.

I call my system *Time Well Spent©* because I believe it is truly that! Time spent teaching your children how to effectively manage their time to become responsible, independent young adults. My children are quickly learning there is always a trade-off between the time and effort it takes to get something done and the reward for having completed the task.

Hopefully, what is learned from *Time Well Spent©* will help my children go out into the world with the disciplines of responsible saving, giving and spending.

So I developed for each child a three-drawer banking system with a magnetic dry-erase board and individualized job magnets. The Bank has one drawer for **SAVING**, one for **GIVING** and one for

SPENDING. Each night, I quickly put up each child's set of job magnets. During the following day, it is each child's responsibility to go to the job chart and remove the magnets when the jobs are completed. At the end of the day, I pay out the monetary reward for completing 100% of the jobs … ALL OR NOTHING. We put 10% of the earned money into each of the **SAVING** and **GIVING** drawers and the remaining 80% into the **SPENDING** drawer.

- The **SAVINGS DRAWER** is not to be touched and when it grows sufficiently will be placed in their first savings account.
- The **GIVING DRAWER** is emptied each week when we attend our church service on Sunday or saved for a charity of choice.
- The **SPENDING DRAWER** is theirs to do with as they please.

Now they understand that everything has a dollar value attached to it and they can rationalize on their own whether or not it is worth their hard-earned money to buy the desired item.

I can only hope, that after all my efforts to guide my children towards good habits with their time and money, when they leave our daily guidance they will be prepared for the journey that awaits them and I can look back and say it was *Time Well Spent*©.

If you would like more information on how to put together your own *Time Well Spent*© system, please email Susan Morrell, at: Time-Well-Spent@comcast. net.

49

Create a Job

After I had been a Plant Manager for a few years, I wanted to get back into a position that would help me achieve my long-term goals of being the head of a division in my company by the time I was 50.

This meant that I had to get back into another management position in the company but there wasn't any kind of job, that I could see, that would match my career goals with my experience and abilities.

I thought, "Why not create such a job and then sell it to the company?"

I had observed that the Vice President of Manufacturing had too many people reporting to him. He had four Area Plant Managers and approximately eight Manufacturing Staff and Services groups directly reporting to him. Twelve groups left a "span of control" much larger than he could effectively manage.

There was no possible way he could give the necessary support and attention to all these groups. Each group vied for his time and would literally stand in line outside his office, waiting their turn to steal a few minutes with him.

I saw an opportunity to solve a problem by creating a position that had all the Manufacturing Staffs and Services groups reporting to one person who in turn would report to the Manufacturing Vice-President ... This would lower his "span of control" to five, a more manageable number.

I convinced him this was a position that he should establish and that I was the right person for the job.

That is how I became the Manager of the Manufacturing Staffs and Services Group, which became an important stepping-stone in fulfilling my long-range goals.

One of the principles in the art of negotiating is to "repackage" the deal. This same technique works in your personal life. Sometimes you just have to create something to fit your goals and desires.

A Simple Lesson in Economics

I never understood how the government or the media could convince the public that a cut in the amount of increase in a program was a "tax cut;" or, a tax decrease should give more to the lower taxpayer and less to the wealthiest taxpayer.

The following short story puts tax cuts in terms that everyone can understand.

Suppose that every day, ten men go out for dinner. The bill for all ten comes to $100. If they pay their bill the way we pay our taxes, it would go something like this:

The first four men (the poorest) would pay nothing
The fifth would pay $1
The sixth would pay $3
The seventh $7
The eighth $12
The ninth $18
The tenth man (the richest) would pay $59

So that's what they decided to do. The ten men ate dinner in the restaurant every day and seemed quite happy with the arrangement, until one day, the owner threw them a curve. "Since you are all such good customers," he said, "I'm going to reduce the cost of your daily meal by $20."

So, now dinner for ten only cost $80. The group still wanted to pay their bill the way we pay our taxes. So, the first four men were unaffected. They would still eat for free. What about the other six, the paying customers? How could they divvy up the $20 windfall so that everyone would get his "fair share?"

The six men realized that $20 divided by six is $3.33. But if they subtracted that from everybody's share, then the fifth man and the sixth man would each end up being "PAID" to eat their meal. So, the restaurant owner suggested that it would be fair to reduce each man's bill by roughly the same amount, and he proceeded to work out the amounts each should pay.

> The fifth man, like the first four, now paid nothing
> The sixth now paid $2 instead of $3 (33% savings).
> The seventh now paid $5 instead of $7 (28% savings).
> The eighth now paid $9 instead of $12 (25% savings).
> The ninth now paid $14 instead of $18 (22% savings).

The tenth now paid $49 instead of $59 (16% savings).

Each of the six was better off than before and the first four continued to eat for free. But once outside the restaurant, the men began to compare their savings.

"I only got a dollar out of the $20," declared the sixth man. He pointed to the tenth man: "but he got $10!"

"Yeah, that's right," exclaimed the fifth man. "I only saved a dollar, too. It's unfair that he got ten times more than me!"

"That's true!" shouted the seventh man. "Why should he get $10 back when I got only $2? The wealthy get all the breaks!"

"Wait a minute," yelled the first four men in unison. "We didn't get anything at all. The System exploits the poor!"

The nine surrounded the tenth and beat him up.

The next night the tenth man didn't show up for dinner, so the nine sat down and ate without him. But when it came time to pay the bill, they discovered something important. They didn't have enough money between all of them for even half of the bill.

That is how our tax system works. The people who pay the highest taxes get the most benefit from a tax reduction. Tax them too much, attack them for being wealthy, and they just may not show up at the table anymore.

Don't ever forget it is our money ... the taxpayers.

ABOUT THE AUTHOR

LAWRENCE J. BEIGHEY

Employed in the manufacturing industry for over twenty-five years, Larry Beighey held various management positions, which gave him a broad, general business background. As President and Chief Operating Officer (COO), he merged two acquisitions into a $150 MM packaging company. He founded Transition Management Resources, a consulting firm that provided management resources to struggling companies. In 1990, he, along with another equity partner, purchased a troubled injection molding company.

His various responsibilities have provided him expertise in all management areas and he has extensive international business experience.

Larry Beighey has taught at the university level and has authored numerous business articles.

In 1988, he was named to WHO'S WHO IN AMERICA.

He is married to Carole La Flamme Beighey, a writer of children's books, and they have six grown children, Skip, Susan, Tom, Tim, Elizabeth and Anne. The Beigheys have ten grandchildren.

He resides with his wife at Amelia Island, Florida and summers at Hubbard Lake, Michigan.

Printed in the United States
76418LV00001B/41